I Think First

Controlling Your Actions

Leigh McClure

SOCIAL AND EMOTIONAL LEARNING FOR THE REAL WORLD™

Rosen Classroom™

I think before I talk.

I think before I cross.

I think before I touch.

I think before I eat.

I think before I choose.

I think first.

Words to Know

cross

touch